1 MONTH OF
FREE
READING

at

www.ForgottenBooks.com

By purchasing this book you are eligible for one month membership to ForgottenBooks.com, giving you unlimited access to our entire collection of over 1,000,000 titles via our web site and mobile apps.

To claim your free month visit:

www.forgottenbooks.com/free912040

ISBN 978-0-266-93403-5
PIBN 10912040

Catalog

of the

Bible Institute

(Formerly known as The Fort Wayne Bible Training School)

Fort Wayne, Indiana

School Board

▼ ▼
▼

Rev. S. J. Grabill, *Chairman* - - Fort Wayne, Indiana

Rev. C. J. Gerig, *Secretary* - - Woodburn, Indiana

Rev. H. E. Tropf - - - - - Berne, Indiana

Rev. A. B. Yoder - - - - - Elkhart, Indiana

Rev. J. K. Gerig - - - - - Chicago, Illinois

Rev. J. A. Ringenberg - - - - Grabill, Indiana

Rev. L. H. Ziemer - - - - - - Toledo, Ohio

Rev. M. N. Amstutz - - - - - Pettisville, Ohio

Mr. S. A. Lehman - - - - Fort Wayne, Indiana

Administration

REV. J. E. RAMSEYER - - - - - - *President*

REV. B. F. LEIGHTNER - - - - - - *Dean*

REV. S. A. WITMER - - - - - - *Registrar*

REV. P. L. EICHER - - *Treasurer and Business Manager*

MISS LILLIAN ZELLER - - - - *Dean of Women*

Trustees

Faculty

REV. J. E. RAMSEYER
Lectures on Deeper Christian Life

REV. B. F. LEIGHTNER
Doctrine and Exposition

REV. BYRON G. SMITH
Bible and Homiletics

REV. JOSHUA STAUFFER
Bible

REV. S. A. WITMER
History and Missions

MISS LILLIAN ZELLER
English

MRS. BYRON G. SMITH
Languages

PROF. C. A. GERBER
Music

PROF. RAYMOND WEAVER
Piano
Student Teacher

MISS MYRA MARTIN R. N.
First Aid

Special Lecturers

1932-1933

REV. PAUL REES,
Evangelist
Detroit, Michigan.

REV. OSWALD J. SMITH,
Director, Russian and Spanish Missions
Toronto, Canada.

REV. JACOB HYGEMA,
Evangelist and Bible Teacher
Fort Wayne, Indiana.

REV. PAUL THOMAS,
General Secretary, Pilgrim Holiness Church
Indianapolis, Indiana.

REV. FORMAN LINCICOME,
Evangelist
Gary, Indiana.

REV. CHARLES STALKER,
Evangelist and Bible Teacher
Columbus, Ohio.

Calendar

1932

SEPTEMBER
S	M	T	W	T	F	S
..	..	..	..	1	2	3
4	5	6	7	8	9	10
11	12	13	14	15	16	17
18	19	20	21	22	23	24
25	26	27	28	29	30	..

NOVEMBER
S	M	T	W	T	F	S
..	..	1	2	3	4	5
6	7	8	9	10	11	12
13	14	15	16	17	18	19
20	21	22	23	24	25	26
27	28	29	30	..	..	..

OCTOBER
S	M	T	W	T	F	S
..	..	..	..	..	..	1
2	3	4	5	6	7	8
9	10	11	12	13	14	15
16	17	18	19	20	21	22
23	24	25	26	27	28	29
30	31	..	..	..	..	..

DECEMBER
S	M	T	W	T	F	S
..	..	..	..	1	2	3
4	5	6	7	8	9	10
11	12	13	14	15	16	17
18	19	20	21	22	23	24
25	26	27	28	29	30	31

1933

JANUARY
S	M	T	W	T	F	S
1	2	3	4	5	6	7
8	9	10	11	12	13	14
15	16	17	18	19	20	21
22	23	24	25	26	27	28
29	30	31	..	..	..	..

MARCH
S	M	T	W	T	F	S
..	..	..	1	2	3	4
5	6	7	8	9	10	11
12	13	14	15	16	17	18
19	20	21	22	23	24	25
26	27	28	29	30	31	..

FEBRUARY
S	M	T	W	T	F	S
..	..	..	1	2	3	4
5	6	7	8	9	10	11
12	13	14	15	16	17	18
19	20	21	22	23	24	25
26	27	28	..	..	..	..

APRIL
S	M	T	W	T	F	S
..	..	..	..	..	..	1
2	3	4	5	6	7	8
9	10	11	12	13	14	15
16	17	18	19	20	21	22
23	24	25	26	27	28	29
30	..	..	..	..	..	..

MAY
S	M	T	W	T	F	S
..	1	2	3	4	5	6
7	8	9	10	11	12	13
14	15	16	17	18	19	20
21	22	23	24	25	26	27
28	29	30	31	..	..	..

First Semester

*September 20, Registration Day.

Service in Chapel, 7:30 p. m.

November 24 to 27, Thanksgiving Vacation.

December 23 to Jan. 2, Holiday Vacation.

Second Semester

January 26, Registration Day.

April 13-17, Easter Vacation.

*May 21, Baccalaureate Sermon, 8:00 p. m.

*May 23, Musical Recital, 8:15 p. m.

*May 24, Fellowship Circle Meeting, 7:30 p. m.

*May 25, Graduation Exercises, 10:30 a. m.

---

*Central Daylight Saving Time.

Our Creed

The Fort Wayne Bible Institute is definitely committed to the conservative and evangelical interpretations of the great doctrines of the Christian faith:

The divine inspiration and consequent authority of the whole canonical Scriptures.

The Trinity of the Godhead—Father, Son, and Holy Spirit.

The fall of man, his consequent moral depravity and the need of regeneration.

The incarnation of Jesus Christ to reveal the Father and to make atonement for the sins of the whole world through His substitutionary death.

Personal salvation by repentance toward God and faith in Jesus Christ.

The baptism with the Holy Spirit as a definite, crisis experience subsequent to conversion for purity in life and power in service.

The imminent, premillennial, second coming of Jesus Christ our Lord.

The resurrection of the body, both in the case of the just and the unjust.

The eternal life of the saved and the eternal punishment of the lost.

While the Bible Institute stands firmly for these truths, it considers the spirit of equal importance to the letter. It lays as much stress on the Christian character of the messenger as upon the orthodox correctness of his message. These fundamentals are held to be essential:

Whole-hearted love toward God and man.
Christian fellowship among believers.
Scriptural separation from the world.
Victory through the indwelling Christ.
Unswerving loyalty to Christ as Lord.
Consecration for rugged, sacrificial service.
Zealous witnessing for Christ.

The leadership of the Holy Spirit for the believer and the church.

A living, working faith in the promises of God for spiritual, physical, and temporal needs.

Historical Sketch

It was in the late summer of 1904 that excavation was begun on the present site of the Fort Wayne Bible Institute. The building was completed in January 1905 and classes were begun in the same month. The institution is, therefore, in its twenty-eighth year.

For more than a quarter of a century hundreds of young people have come to her halls and have lighted their torches at her altars to go out to the dark portions of the earth holding forth the Word of Life. The Institution was born from the vision, sacrifice, and work of its founders; and those very essentials have characterized its life since.

The antecedent of the Fort Wayne Bible Training School was known as Bethany Home, in Bluffton, Ohio. Prompted by an implicit faith in God's Word, a few godly people conducted this home as a retreat for the sick who were seeking the Great Physician, and as a haven for Christian workers needing rest and recuperation. In a few years the scope of the vision was enlarged to include teaching of the Bible. Then it became known as Bethany Institute.

Later the increased demand for Bible training led to definite steps to enlarge its quarters and extend its service. The institution then passed into the hands of the Missionary Church Association. This body selected a beautiful site at the edge of Fort Wayne, Indiana, and founded the Bible Training School. The school operated under this name until the year 1930, when the name was changed to The Fort Wayne Bible Institute. This change of name, however, does not indicate any change in the character of the institution, which always has been interdenominational. Several different denominations are represented on its board and its teaching staff, and students from eighteen to twenty denominations are in attendance each year.

To meet growing demands and to measure up to increasing opportunities it became necessary about three years ago to provide greater dormitory and classroom facilities. Accordingly, a beautiful new building, providing attractive, pleasant dormitory rooms and adequate class rooms, was erected at a cost of $60,-000. This is the women's dormitory and is known as Bethany Hall.

Location

The Fort Wayne Bible Institute is admirably situated. According to the 1930 census the center of the population of the United States is just west of the city of Fort Wayne. It is also at the very hub of the industrial Middle West. Within a radius of three hundred and fifty miles are Chicago, Detroit, Cleveland, Cincinnati, St. Louis, Indianapolis, Milwaukee, Toledo, and Pittsburgh. Fort Wayne is readily accessible from all these points; several trunk lines pass through the city, and bus and interurban lines radiate from this center.

The Institute is located in the southwest section of Fort Wayne, surrounded by the finest residential district in the city. The buildings stand in a spacious grove of native trees, removed from the noise and soot of the industrial section, yet easily accessible by street-car from all parts of the city. The campus of three and a half acres provides room for healthful recreation. If more room is desired it is within easy reach, for a few blocks west lies beautiful Foster Park along the St. Mary's River. The thoroughfare between the school and the park is Rudisill Boulevard, the main east-and-west traffic artery of south Ft. Wayne.

Purpose

The objective of the Institute is to instruct men and women in the Word of God, which is the foundation of our spiritual heritage, and to train them for the service which has been committed to the church of Jesus Christ. Finding a place in the imperial program for the evangelization of the world is the privilege of every disciple, yet this vision involves thorough preparation whether the call be for home or foreign work.

However, many students do not have a definite call to Christian work, yet desire a thorough knowledge of the Word of God. This school aims to so emphasize the great fundamentals of faith and the deeper life through the indwelling of the Holy Spirit that the teaching shall be translated literally into the lives of the students. The study of the Scriptures is given first place in all courses. Approximately one-half of the time devoted to all subjects in the courses of study is spent upon the divinely inspired Word of God.

Devotional Life

This institution has provided carefully for the devotional culture of its students. The constant endeavor is to make the school a home with such a spiritual atmosphere as shall develop the habits of a prayer life, which are so essential to fruitful service.

The day is begun with "quiet hour", a period of private devotion before breakfast. All classes are opened by prayer. The mid-morning chapel service provides an interim for spiritual inspiration. At five o'clock the men and women meet in their respective groups for a half hour of missionary intercession. In accordance with their weekly schedule the globe is encircled by prayer. Following supper, evening worship affords opportunity for expressions of prayer and praise in song and testimony. The half day which is set aside each month for prayer has proved invaluable in heart searching, cleansing, and filling. This continual spiritual exercise is bound to foster the building of true Christian character.

The Library

The Library is a vital factor in the work of the Institute. It has been steadily enlarged year by year by books carefully selected for their relation to our Academic, Missionary, and Theological Courses. On the shelves are found books of general information, books affording material for collateral reading and books which furnish a source for research work. A nominal sum of one dollar per term is paid by each student for the use of the library.

Practical Christian Service

An invaluable aid in the training of the Christian worker is practical service. This particular factor is just as important to him as the laboratory is to the scientist. Practical Christian service brings the classroom in direct contact with the everyday problems relating to the promulgation of the Gospel; accordingly, it furnishes the best possible motive for thorough study.

In harmony with the law in the spiritual realm, that one receives spiritual impulses only as he shares them with others, this practical phase of the training furnishes the student with the proper outlet for the inspiration received through the Institute. Practical Christian service teaches to do by doing, but apart from the pure experience it affords, it involves a solemn responsibility which is reflected in every department of the institution.

Every student is required to engage in at least six hours of practical work per week, averaging two assignments. These are assigned to him carefully in accordance with his previous training, experience, and individual preferences in view of his future work. The appointment of students to these various services as well as all other matters pertaining to this department is in charge of the Practical Work Committee.

Fort Wayne offers unique advantages for practical Christian service. It is largely an industrial city with a population of 115,000 according to the latest census. There are also numerous fields of service among the adjacent rural communities, nearby towns, and lesser cities. The Bible Institute is the only institution of its kind within the city or a wide radius thereof.

Of the various calls for practical Christian work which have come to us, Sunday School teaching stands foremost. There has been a growing demand for our students as teachers in the city churches. For more than a score of years our students have had sole charge of a Sunday School at the County Children's Home. Through the faithful teaching of the Word many of these unfortunate and often uncared-for children have been led to the Saviour. When the weather is favorable, a voluntary and enthusiastic group of students conduct street meetings down town in the heart of the business section. On Saturday night some teams of men visit such nondescript rendezvous as drink parlors and pool halls to distribute tracts and occasionally drop a word for the Master. Visiting the sick in hospitals and needy homes is as much an inlet for divine blessing upon the visitors as an outlet for divine compassion upon the visited. Thus wherever a student whose heart is aglow meets a hungry soul a contact for the gospel story is made.

In connection with the religious work carried on by the local Y. M. C. A., the students have had exceptional and numerous opportunities to sing the Gospel at the shops and factories of the city. Since this work is in charge of the Religious Secretary of the Y. M. C. A., we have no means of tabulating the results, but from the oral reports received we are assured that God's blessing has attended this ministry.

The following reports will give a general idea of the extent of definite work accomplished by students during the school year of 1930-31. Approximately 1,300 Sunday School classes were taught; 325 services were conducted; 530 services were addressed; 550 homes were visited; 1,200 persons were dealt with individually; and 700 accepted Christ as their personal Saviour.

Gospel Teams

One noteworthy branch of the Practical Work Department is that of the Gospel Teams. Under the signal favor of God, this method of evangelization has afforded students splendid experience and has brought the happiness of the full Gospel to many hearts. The character of its ministry is primarily evangelistic. Students do not go out to advertise the Institute directly, but to honor Christ in song, testimony, and in the preaching of the Word. A regular team consists of an organized quartet of singers and a speaker.

The teams minister chiefly in denominational churches within a radius of two hundred miles of Fort Wayne. The personnel of a team depends upon the requirements of a particular assignment. Sometimes a church desires singers only; again, a pastor wants his pulpit supplied for a Sunday; or a young people's society want a team to render a missionary program. Many local churches have called on the teams to assist them in protracted evangelistic services.

The work of the gospel teams has grown steadily since its inception in 1924. About twenty-five students were engaged in this form of practical Christian service during the past year. In this number there were three male quartets and two ladies' quartets. Some of the more distant points visited by teams include Detroit and Brown City, Michigan; Groveland, Seneca, and Peoria, Illinois; Pewaukee, Wisconsin; and Cleveland, Ohio.

Reports for 1931-32, the last year for which complete statistics are available, indicate that gospel teams served in 307 services. 1,211 songs and 131 addresses were given, and 232 were reported to have accepted Christ. The total per-student mileage would more than encircle the earth twice: it approximated 60,000 miles.

Churches from the following denominations enjoyed the ministry of the teams: Evangelical, Christian, Pilgrim Holiness, Baptist, Presbyterian, Methodist Episcopal, United Brethren, Wesleyan Methodist, Christian Union, Church of God, Methodist Protestant, Friends, Mennonite Brethren in Christ, Christian and Missionary Alliance, African M. E., Missionary Church Association, Defenseless Mennonite, besides several city missions.

Mission Band

Institutions of learning usually have their fraternal and literary societies. The Bible Institute does not have these. Its chief student organization is a society known as the Students' Mission Band. This is an aggressive society organized to create and stimulate interest in world-wide missions. It includes every student, and is largely responsible for the distinctive missionary atmosphere which pervades the Institute. Putting ideals into practice, this society has assumed the sole support of Mr. Clayton Steiner, a graduate of the Bible Institute, now serving as missionary in Peru, South America. Each Friday evening the students of the Mission Band conduct a public missionary service, and by divine providence many choice missionaries from India, Afghanistan, Tibet, China, Japan, South America, the Philippine Islands, Armenia, Palestine, Russia, and other countries have addressed these meetings, firing anew the missionary zeal which burned in the hearts of the students. This society also has charge of evening prayer meetings, the weekly schedule of which includes every mission field.

Broadcasting Over WOWO

Students have been given repeated opportunities of broadcasting over WOWO, Indiana's strongest radio station. While the Institute hasn't had a regular period in its own name, yet its representatives have appeared by invitation on such programs as the Misionary Hour and the services of the Fort Wayne Gospel Temple. It is hoped that the Institute will have a regular period of broadcasting beginning with September, 1932, in order to teach, preach and sing the gospel to many who would not otherwise hear it.

The Light Tower

The Light Tower is the name of the yearbook which is published by the student body of the Institute. Thus far it has been a biennial publication, editions having been published in 1928, 1930, and 1932. The book aims to portray the life of the school and it serves as a memorial of "Bible school days" to graduates. It is an attractive book that reflects credit to the creative ability of its editors and managers. It is by no means an improvised imitation of a college or high school annual. It is designed to reflect the unique atmosphere and life of the Bible Institute.

World-Wide Missions At the F. W. B. I.

One hundred years ago the church was awakening to its long-lost responsibility of world evangelization. The missionary movement then begun has reached almost world-wide proportions. The demands of this growing enterprise required centers of training for young men and women, and Bible schools were accordingly established. Simultaneously with the growth of the missionary movement came the breakdown of many seminaries in the essential task of *teaching the Word of God*. But the great heart cry that rose from the pagan world was not for Western civilization, education or philosophy, but the message of Life and Redemption that is found in the Book.

The question may be asked—one that suggests the true measure of a school's worth—"What are its students doing?" The answer to that question will show that the Bible Institute has made a modest but distinct contribution to world-wide missions. Its graduates are busy in the great world of life. Theirs is an altruism that knows no extreme of climate, distinction of race nor national boundary as a barrier to their task. The cold Tibetan highlands, the teeming provinces of China, the hot plains of India, the sultry tropics of Africa, the lofty Andes of South America, the picturesque islands of Hawaii, our own Indian reservations and Southern mountain districts are among the scenes of their labors of mercy.

In addition to the foreign missionaries indicated above, approximately two hundred of its alumni are engaged in home pastorates, and a considerable number in other forms of Christian service.

Courses Offered

The Institute offers four courses of study—the Standard Bible Course, the Two-Year Bible Course, the Academic-Bible Course, and the Bible-Music Course.

I. THE STANDARD BIBLE COURSE—THREE YEARS

This is the standard course intended for those who desire to become pastors, evangelists, missionaries, Sunday School, or lay workers. Ninety-six hours are required for graduation. Twenty of these are electives, and the student may therefore specialize in a particular department in view of his future field of service. If he intends to become a missionary, History of Missions, Missionary Principles and Practices, Non-Christian Religions, First Aid, and one of the romance languages are recommended as electives. If he intends to become a pastor, such subjects as Pastoral Work, Public Speaking, and Christian Ethics should be chosen. Women are advised to elect Personal Work, First Aid, Deaconess Course, The Process of Teaching, and Child Study. Five of the elected credits may be chosen from the Department of Music.

The requirements are as follows:

Bible	45 credits
Church History	4 credits
Apologetics	4 credits
Homiletics (for men)	6 credits
Deaconess Course (for women)	4 credits
Service	4 credits
*English	6 credits
Music I and III	7 credits
Electives	20 credits

*Students may be exempt from this subject if they satisfactorily pass an examination or submit college credits.

Entrance requirements: It is preferred that students be high school graduates. However, applicants who have satisfactorily completed two years of English and at least one year of Ancient or Modern History in high school will be admitted to the course. Men must be 18 years of age and women 17. This age limit does not apply to high school graduates.

II. THE BIBLE COURSE—TWO YEARS

This course is designed for advance students who desire the unique advantages of Bible Study and character building afforded by the Bible Institute, but who for various reasons do not want the more extensive standard three year course. An increasing number of college students, or high school graduates who intend to take college work later, avail themselves of this course. Sixty-four credits are required for graduation, eight of which may be from the Department of Music.

The requirements are as follows:

Bible	38 credits
Church History or Missions I	4 credits
Apologetics	2 credits
Homiletics	6 credits
Music I and III	6 credits
Electives	8 credits

Entrance requirements: Graduation from high school with satisfactory level of attainment and ability.

III. THE ACADEMIC BIBLE COURSE—FOUR YEARS

This course is intended for those who have not had a high school education and can therefore not enter the regular courses outlined above. The course combines high school work in English and History with the Standard Bible Course. The first year is devoted to a study of English Grammar, Composition, Oral Interpretation, Orthography, and Bible I. In the second year the student continues his study of English in rhetoric and composition. He also studies General History and advances in Bible -studies. The third and fourth years run practically parallel to the second and third years of the Standard Bible Course. A total of 128 credits are required for graduation, 14 of which may be from the Department of Music.

The requirements are as follows:

Bible	45 credits
Apologetics	4 credits
Homiletics	6 credits
Service	4 credits
Music I and III	8 credits
Church History	4 credits
General History	4 credits
English	28 credits
Electives	23 credits

Entrance requirements: Applicants must be 17 years of age. They should have a working knowledge of the English language.

IV. THE BIBLE-MUSIC COURSE

The purpose of this course is to train men and women for gospel singing, choir directing, piano playing, and hymn writing. Students desiring to graduate from this course are required to take 24 hours of Bible, including Bible I (Old Testament), Bible II (Gospels), Bible III (Acts and Epistles), and Bible XII. In addition to this they must complete all the class instruction in music and take no fewer than two private lessons each week. With each voice lesson one hour of consistent practice is required each day. With each piano lesson one and one-half hours of practice are required daily. The private work may consist of two piano lessons, or two vocal lessons, or one of each per week. A student must pursue piano or voice for at least one year in order to receive credit for graduation.

Persons majoring in voice are required to earn two credits in Music II and also in Music IV. Those majoring in piano will only be required to earn one credit in each of these subjects. Students taking this course may elect any other subjects from the departments of Bible, History, Missions, Philosophy, Apologetics, Languages, English, Homiletics. and Public Speaking, and Service. Sixty-four term hour credits are required for graduation.

The requirements are as follows:

Bible _____ 24 credits
Music (class instruction) _____ 14 to 16 credits
Music (private) _____ 16 to 24 credits
Electives _____ 2 to 8 credits

Entrance requirements: It is preferred that applicants be high school graduates. However, applicants who have satisfactorily completed 2 years of English in high school will be admitted to the course. Men must be 18 years of age and women 17. This age limit does not apply to high school graduates.

Special Courses

Special courses may be arranged for students who do not wish to enter the regular graduate courses. Studies may be selected in keeping with the previous training and future needs of the student. The Registrar and the Dean are glad to advise students regarding courses of study, and they seek to arrange the schedule of a student on the basis of his individual needs.

ENTRANCE TO BETHANY HALL

ADMINISTRAT.

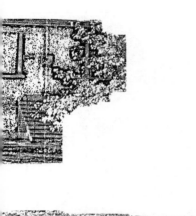

BUILDING

STUDENT'S ROOM

General Entrance Requirements

Every applicant must be a Christian in character.

Credit will be given for equivalent work satisfactorily done in other schools of recognized merit. Students who desire advanced standing upon the basis of work completed in other schools are advised to present their credits when entering.

Students enrolling for full time work must be able to carry at least twelve hours per week. A maximum of nineteen hours per week is permitted, although the maximum may be less than that in the case of students who must spend a considerable amount of time in self-help or other responsibilities. Students who cannot do justice to their studies on account of extra- curricular tasks are advised to extend their courses over an additional year.

Standard Bible Course --- 3 Years

FIRST YEAR

FIRST TERM

	Periods per Week
Bible I—Old Testament	4
Bible II—New Testament—Gospels	4
Service	2
**English VI	3
Music I—Notation	2
Music III—General Chorus	1
***Electives	

SECOND TERM

Bible I—Old Testament	4
Bible III—New Testament—Acts and Epistles	4
Service	2
**English VI	3
Music I—Notation	2
Music III—General Chorus	1
***Electives	

SECOND YEAR

FIRST TERM

*Bible VII—Romans and Galatians 4
*Bible V—The Poetical Books 3
Bible XII—Doctrine 2
History II—Church History 2
Music III—General Chorus 1
***Electives ....

SECOND TERM

*Bible VI—Old Testament Prophets 4
*Bible IX—The Pastoral Epistles 3
Bible XII—Doctrine 2
History II—Church History 2
Music III—General Chorus 1
***Electives ....

THIRD YEAR

FIRST TERM

*Bible IV—The Pentateuch 4
*Bible X—The General Epistles 3
Bible XII—Doctrine 2
Apologetics 2
Homiletics 3
Music III—General Chorus 1
***Electives ....

SECOND TERM

*Bible VIII—The Church Epistles 4
*Bible XI—The Apocalypse 3
Bible XII—Doctrine 2
Apologetics 2
Homiletics 3
Music III—General Chorus 1
***Electives ....

*Twenty-one credits must be earned in these Bible subjects.

**Those who pass an entrance examination successfully in this subject may elect something else in its stead.

***Enough electives must be carried to make the required credits for graduation. At least twenty-two must be earned during the three years.

The Bible Course --- 2 Years

FIRST YEAR

FIRST TERM

	Periods per Week
Bible I—Old Testament	4
Bible II—New Testament—Gospels	4
Bible XII—Doctrine	2
History II—Church History or Missions I—History of Missions	2
Music I—Notation	2
Music III—General Chorus	1
Electives	

SECOND TERM

Bible I—Old Testament	4
Bible III—New Testament—Acts and Epistles	4
Bible XII—Doctrine	2
History II—Church History or Missions I—History of Missions	2
Music I—Notation	2
Music III—General Chorus	1
Electives	

SECOND YEAR

FIRST TERM

Bible VII—Romans and Galatians	4
Bible V—The Poetical Books	3
Bible XII—Doctrine	2
Homiletics	3
Apologetics	2
Music II—General Chorus	1
Electives	

SECOND TERM

Bible VI—Prophets, (Old Testament)	4
Bible IX—The Pastoral Epistles	3
Bible XII—Doctrine	2
Homiletics	3
Music III—General Chorus	1
Electives	

The Bible-Music Course --- 2 Years

FIRST YEAR

FIRST TERM

Periods per Week

Bible I—Old Testament	4
Bible XII—Doctrine	2
Music I—Notation	2
Music II—Sight Reading	1
Music III—General Chorus	1
Music IV—Conducting	1
Music VII or VIII—Voice or Piano	2
Electives	

SECOND TERM

Bible I—Old Testament	4
Bible XII—Doctrine	2
Music I—Notation	2
Music II—Sight Reading	1
Music III—General Chorus	1
Music IV—Conducting	1
Music VII or VIII—Voice or Piano	2
Electives	

SECOND YEAR

FIRST TERM

Bible II—New Testament—Gospels	4
Bible XII—Doctrine	2
Music III—General Chorus	1
Music V—Harmony	2
Music VII or VIII—Voice or Piano	2
Music IX—Normal Training	1
Electives	

SECOND TERM

Bible III—New Testament—Acts and Epistles	4
Bible XII—Doctrine	2
Music III—General Chorus	1
Music VI—Composition	2
Music VII or VIII—Voice or Piano	2
Music IX—Normal Training	1
Electives	

The Academic Bible Course --- 4 Years

FIRST YEAR

FIRST TERM

	Periods per Week
Bible I—Old Testament	4
English I—Orthography	3
English III—English Grammar	3
English IV—Composition	3
Music I—Notation	2
Music III—General Chorus	1
Electives	

SECOND TERM

Bible I—Old Testament	4
English II—Oral Interpretation	3
English III—English Grammar	3
English IV—Composition	3
Music I—Notation	2
Music III—General Chorus	1
Electives	

SECOND YEAR

FIRST TERM

Bible II—New Testament—Gospels	4
Bible XII—Doctrine	2
Service	2
English V—Rhetoric	3
History I—General History	3
Music III—General Chorus	1
Electives	

SECOND TERM

Bible III—New Testament—Acts and Epistles	4
Bible XII—Doctrine	2
Service	2
English V—Rhetoric	3
History I—General History	3
Music III—General Chorus	1
Electives	

THIRD YEAR
First Term

*Bible VII—Romans and Galatians _____ 4
*Bible V—The Poetical Books _____ 3
Bible XII—Doctrine _____ 2
History II—Church History _____ 2
English VI _____ 3
Music III—General Chorus _____ 1
Electives _____

Second Term

*Bible VI—Old Testament Prophets _____ 4
*Bible IX—The Pastoral Epistles _____ 3
Bible XII—Doctrine _____ 2
History II—Church History _____ 2
English VI _____ 3
Music III—General Chorus _____ 1
Electives _____

FOURTH YEAR
First Term

*Bible IV—The Pentateuch _____ 4
*Bible X—The General Epistles _____ 3
Apologetics _____ 2
Homiletics _____ 3
Music III—General Chorus _____ 1
Electives _____

Second Term

*Bible VIII—The Church Epistles _____ 4
*Bible XI—The Apocalypse _____ 3
Apologetics _____ 2
Homiletics _____ 3
Music III—General Chorus _____ 1
Electives _____

*Twenty-one credits must be earned in these Bible subjects.

Description of Subjects
Bible

BIBLE I—OLD TESTAMENT. This is an introductory study of the Old Testament which is designed to prepare the student for the more advanced courses in the Pentateuch, the Prophecies, and the Poetical Books. The books are taken up in the order in which they were written and all are surveyed and outlined. The principle of organization of the subject-matter is the history of divine revelation from Creation to Christ. The geographical background of the narrative is also treated. This course combines therefore in one co-ordinated unit the common studies offered in Synthetic Bible, History, and Geography. Required in all Courses. Value, 8 term hours.

BIBLE II—THE GOSPELS. A study of the four Gospels. In the approach to the life of Christ the providential preparation of the world for the Messiah and the historical background are considered. The person and work of Christ are studied and the peculiar characteristics of each book are noted. This is a unified course which aims to set forth the complete biography of our Lord with the necessary geographical and historical detail. In this subject there are unusual advantages to study the messages and the art of the world's master Teacher. Required in all Courses. Value, 4 term hours.

BIBLE III—THE ACTS AND THE EPISTLES. This is an introductory study to the latter half of the New Testament. It follows Bible II and continues the study of Christ as the ascended Lord operating through the church by the Holy Spirit. The history of the early church, the missionary journeys of the Apostle Paul, and the labors of other Apostles are noted. The historical setting and the structure of the church letters, the general and pastoral epistles are shown. This course prepares the student for the more advanced expositional studies in Bible VII-XI. Required in all Courses. Value, 4 term hours.

BIBLE IV—PENTATEUCH. An advanced study of this important section of the Word of God which is most frequently attacked by modern enemies. It includes a study of creation and the flood in the light of modern research; of the beginnings and early dispensations of human history; of the types foreshadowing God's method of redemption as revealed in the New Testament; and an analysis of each book with practical spiritual applications. Value, 4 term hours. Offered in 1933-34.

BIBLE V—POETICAL BOOKS. A survey is made of the whole section which embraces Job, Psalms, Proverbs, Ecclesiastes, Song of Solomon, and Lamentations. Special emphasis is given to Job and the Psalms, which represent the zenith of Hebrew poetry. The great truths that are revealed regarding suffering and God's providence in the matchless drama of Job are discovered. The Psalms are classified, their origin and ancient usage noted, their prophetical significance and experiential value emphasized. Value, 3 term hours. Offered in 1932-33.

BIBLE VI—OLD TESTAMENT PROPHETS. While one or more of the prophetic books will be treated quite exhaustively, the entire section from Isaiah to Malachi is studied, noting the two-fold character of the messages of the prophets: first, as applying to the times when the prophets lived; second, as referring to future events in the divine plan. Special attention is given to those predictions relating to Christ's first and second advents, Israel's future, the tribulation and the millennium. Value, 4 term hours. Offered in 1932-33.

BIBLE VII—ROMANS AND GALATIANS. An exposition of these epistles. In the former the logical unfolding of the great doctrines of sin, salvation and sanctification are studied. Special attention is also given to the chapters relating to God's plan for Israel, and to the believer's obligation to God, to government and to his fellowmen. In the latter the relation of law and grace and the great doctrine of justification by faith apart from works are shown. Value, 4 term hours. Offered in 1932-33.

BIBLE VIII—THE CHURCH EPISTLES. An advanced study of I and II Corinthians, Ephesians, Philippians, Colossians, I and II Thessalonians. Each book will be analyzed and its distinctive message discovered, and one or more will receive thorough treatment. Value, 4 term hours. Offered in 1933-34.

BIBLE IX—PASTORAL EPISTLES. An expository study giving special attention to the doctrinal and practical aspects of these epistles with special reference to their bearing upon modern pastoral problems. The nature of the organization of the New Testament church, its growth and development, its missionary spirit as revealed in these letters are also given attention. Value, 3 term hours. Offered in 1932-33.

BIBLE X—GENERAL EPISTLES. By analysis and exegesis the teachings of this section of the New Testament are set forth as they relate to doctrine, and to the everyday problems of Christian living. Value, 3 term hours. Offered in 1933-34.

BIBLE XI—THE APOCALYPSE. This course consists of an exposition of the Book of Revelation, following the outline indicated in verse nineteen of chapter one. The predictions found therein are interpreted in the light of Old Testament prophecy, history and current events. While the prophetic element is kept prominent, the devotional and practical value of the book is also emphasized. Value, 3 term hours. Offered in 1933-34.

BIBLE XII—BIBLE DOCTRINE. An invaluable course in these days of apostasy to establish the student in "the most holy faith." The following cardinal doctrines of the Scriptures are studied: the Bible, God, Christ, the Holy Spirit, Man, Sin, Salvation, Church, Angels and Satan, and the Last Things. Text: Pardington's "Outline Studies in Christian Doctrine." Required in all graduate Courses. Value, 8 term hours.

BIBLE XIV—BIBLICAL INTERPRETATION. The general plan of this course is adapted to meet what appears to be the practical wants of students of Theology. Its purpose is to familiarize the student with the methods and principles involved in the correct interpretation of the Scriptures. Elective. Value, 2 term hours.

History

HISTORY I—GENERAL HISTORY. A study of history reveals to us the dealings of God with man and enables us, by a knowledge of the past, to understand better our duty to the present. The study of General History furnishes a foundation for other courses in history and allied subjects. This correlation and God's Providence in the world are kept in view. Text: Meyer's General History. Required in Academic Bible Course unless equivalent credits can be presented. Value, 6 term hours.

HISTORY II—CHURCH HISTORY. A course in the history of the church from the days of the apostles to the present time. A complete outline of church history is given, emphasizing the important matters, and showing how God in the midst of the darkest periods of the church has had a company of His own people who were true to Him to keep alive the true faith. Required in Standard and Academic Bible Course. Value, 4 term hours.

Missions

MISSIONS I—HISTORY OF MISSIONS. A survey of the progress of missionary extension from its inception to the beginning of the modern era is first made. The greater part of the course deals with the modern era: a study of the individual fields, the general facts, the work accomplished, the outstanding problems, and immediate needs of each. It is a comprehensive study of Missions, but not so technical as to neutralize the inspiration to be derived from this important subject. Text: "The Progress of Worldwide Missions"—Glover. Required in Standard and Academic Bible Courses. Value, 4 term hours.

MISSIONS II—MISSIONARY PRINCIPLES AND PRACTICES. An invaluable course for all prospective missionaries. Required by some mission boards of candidates. It treats of such themes as missionary administration and support, the qualifications of missionaries, and other problems of practical value. A special study is made of the principles of self-government, self-support, and self-propagation of the native church. Text: Brown's "The Misionary." Elective. Offered in 1932-33. Value, 2 term hours.

MISSIONS III—NON-CHRISTIAN RELIGIONS. This study consists of an interpretation of the great religions of the world, as well as a presentation of such facts concerning their origin and history as one needs to interpret them rightly. This is all to the one end that the superlative elements of the only true religion of Christ may be set forth and emphasized. Elective. Offered in 1933-34. Value, 2 term hours.

Philosophy

PHILOSOPHY I—CHRISTIAN PHILOSOPHY. A course intended to fortify the student against destructive philosophical skepticism and superstitious credulity. By a series of demonstrations, Christianity is shown to be the true religion and the only religion possible to meet the spiritual wants of mankind. Elective. Value, 2 term hours.

PHILOSOPHY II—CHRISTIAN ETHICS. This course treats both the theoretical and practical aspects of the subject. The source and the principles of the Christian ideal are studied and contrasted with the humanistic theories. The latter part of the course deals with the application of the Christian standard to the complex problems of life. A timely course in this day of confusion of right and wrong. Text: "A Manual of Christian Ethics"—Keyser. Elective. Value, 2 term hours.

Apologetics

APOLOGETICS I—CHRISTIAN EVIDENCES. The purpose of this course is to set the proofs of Christianity before the student that he may be grounded in the fundamental truths of the Word, and be enabled to meet the assaults of the modernist. Text: "A System of Christian Evidences"—Keyser. Elective. Value, 2 term hours.

APOLOGETICS II—GENERAL INTRODUCTION. A study of the canon in its origin, extent, arrangement, and preservation. A historical study of the principal manuscripts and versions leads to the consideration of the English Bible in its popular and critical editions. Text and collateral reading. Alternates with Apologetics III. Offered in 1933-34. Elective. Value, 2 term hours.

APOLOGETICS III—SPECIAL INTRODUCTION. A course which deals with the individual books, considering their authorship, date, and purpose. The revived assaults against the Bible, and particularly against the Old Testament, make the subject timely and helpful. The Mosaic authorship of the Pentateuch, the unity of the book of Isaiah, the authenticity of Daniel are among the conservative positions defended. Text and collateral reading. Alternates with Apologetics II. Offered in 1932-33. Elective. Value, 2 term hours.

Languages

GREEK I—Since Greek was the language chosen by our Lord as the suitable channel to give His highest revelation to mankind, its study is a valuable asset to any student of the Word. The first year is spent largely on grammar and vocabulary as found in "Huddilston's Essentials." Elective. Value, 6 term hours.

GREEK II—The second year is devoted to the study of syntax and selected readings from various New Testament books. The necessary books are "Huddilston's Essentials," a New Testament Greek text, and a good Greek Lexicon of the N. T., preferably Thayer's. Elective. Value, 4 term hours.

SPANISH I—A course in elementary Spanish, including Spanish grammar, reading, and composition. Elective. Value, 6 term hours.

FRENCH I—Elementary French includes French grammar, composition, reading, and translation. First year French, from the beginning lessons, develops classroom and practical conversational use of the language. Elective. Value, 6 term hours.

ENGLISH I—Orthography. This course is a study in word etymology, phonics, and spelling. It provides for a study of the meanings and use of words, their correct and effective pronunciation, and their spelling. In the latter part of the course theological terms are studied. Value, 3 term hours. Required in Academic Bible Course.

ENGLISH II—Oral Interpretation. This course is designed to teach the student the fundamental principles of expression. There is much practice on standard literature to secure clear and distinct utterance, variety of inflection and emphasis, and naturalness of manner. Special attention is given to the reading of Scripture in public. Value, 3 term hours. Required in Academic Bible Course.

ENGLISH III—A thorough course in English Grammar. The aim of the study is threefold: to prepare the student for advanced English, to form the habits of correct speech, and to gain an insight into the principles of the English language. Since a mastery of English is invaluable in acquiring a foreign language, a number of students have elected English III to this end. Text: "Burleson's English Grammar." Required in Bible Academic Course. Value, 6 term hours.

ENGLISH IV.—This course in composition aims to lay a foundation of "Sentence sense" which will enable the student to build well-constructed themes. It insists on the application of Grammar for sentence-improvement and offers many devices for the development of style in writing. Required in the Academic Bible Course. Value, 6 term hours.

ENGLISH V—An advanced course giving thorough instruction in the principles and practice of rhetoric and composition. An effort is made to improve the quality of English from an utilitarian standpoint. Text: "Composition and Rhetoric"— Tanner. Required in the second year of the Academic Bible Courses. Value, 6 term hours.

ENGLISH VI—This course is equivalent to the first year of college English. The object is to familiarize the student with the forms and principles of correct writing. A weekly theme is required of all students. Required in Standard and Academic Bible Courses. Value, 6 term hours.

Homiletics and Public Speaking

HOMILETICS—This course deals with the preparation and delivery of sermons. It aims to acquaint the student with the principles by which this two-fold object may be accomplished. Exercises in sermon construction constitute a considerable part of the class work. The importance of relying upon the definite guidance and illumination of the Holy Spirit in the ministry of God's Word is ever emphasized. Text: "The Preparation and Delivery of Sermons"—Broadus. Required of men in Bible Courses. Value, 6 term hours.

PUBLIC SPEAKING—This course is largely a study of the fundamental qualities of delivery. Its aim is the formation of correct speech habits, and it is intended to meet the question that many students ask, "How is it possible for me to improve my speech?" Elective. Value, 2 term hours.

Service

SERVICE I—PERSONAL WORK. A course designed to aid the Christian in the art of soul winning. The student is taught how to deal with different classes of men and women. Value, 2 term hours. Elective.

SERVICE II—PASTORAL WORK. This study deals with the ministry of the Christian worker outside the pulpit, including the oversight of all the divinely instituted offices of the church and the best methods of conducting the different services. Value, 2 term hours. Elective. Offered in 1932-33.

SERVICE III—THE PROCESS OF TEACHING. This course deals with the fundamental principles of teaching and the typical methods which may be used in Bible School work. A study of the pedagogy of Jesus is made with a two-fold aim: to see how He taught and to apply His methods. Value, 2 term hours. Elective. Offered in 1933-34.

SERVICE IV—CHILD STUDY. This course deals with the normal growth and development of the child, tracing the outstanding characteristics through the different periods of the unfolding life. A study is made of the forces of life building as well as the phases and fields of the religious education of the child. Value, 2 term hours. Elective. Offered in 1932-33.

SERVICE V—EVANGELISM. This course is built up around the idea of practical rather than professional evangelism. The elements essential to revivals, the relation between pastor and evangelist, the evangelist himself, and the conducting of meetings are among the subjects treated. Elective. Value, 2 term hours.

SERVICE VI—FIRST AID. This course is not designed to substitute for courses either in nursing or medicine. It aims to give the student a practical knowledge: 1. Of the human body, 2. Diseases and departures from the normal functions, 3. Emergency care of the sick or injured, 4. A brief study of the common contagious diseases and diseases peculiar to each mission field. All this is only to furnish the worker another contact for presenting the Gospel. Elective. Value, 4 term hours.

Music

MUSIC I—NOTATION. The rudiments of music. In the first term the structure of the major keys and the various symbols are studied; in the second term the chromatic tones, accidentals, intervals, and minor keys are taken up. Text: Towner's "Class and Chorus." Required in both graduate courses. Value, 4 term hours.

MUSIC II—SIGHT READING. Designed to enable the student to read music at sight. Ear training, including the attendant phases of articulation and phrasing, and study of rhythms. Required in the Bible-Music Course. Value, 1 term hour.

MUSIC III—GENERAL CHORUS. This course trains in chorus singing, art of expression, diction, and interpretation. Required in all courses in every year. Value, 1 term hour.

MUSIC IV—CONDUCTING. This course includes the technique of choral conducting, and leading of congregations; the correct and approved way of beating time and method of conveying rhythms, dynamics, and interpretation through the baton. Required in the Bible-Music Course. Value, 1 term hour.

MUSIC V—HARMONY. A study of the formation of chords with their progressions and resolutions, preparing the student for the advanced course in composition. Required in Bible-Music Course. Value, 2 term hours.

MUSIC VI—COMPOSITION. Advanced study in chord formation, counterpoint and composition of songs and their adaptation to selected words. Required in Bible-Music Course. Value, 2 term hours.

MUSIC VII—Private voice culture includes voice building, care and use of voice, proper tone production and placement, breathing, phrasing, and interpretation. Students in the Bible Course electing one lesson per week will be required to practice one-half hour per day. One credit will be allowed for a term's work. Students in the Bible-Music Course will be allowed two credits for a term's work, due to a double amount of practice required.

Music VIII—In private piano instruction emphasis is laid on a thorough technical foundation. All students are prepared carefully in scales (thirds, sixths, eighths, tenths; in staccato, contrary motion, and cannon), arpeggios in all forms and touches, and octaves. This background combined with the classics and additional exercise material develops hymn playing, eliminating the difficulties of playing hymns in any key. Hymns are studied from the standpoint of pedaling, time, rapid reading, and transposition.

Music IX—Normal Training. This course is designed to train the student to teach the theory of music. It is a self-evident fact that it is one thing to train a pupil in the technique of music, and quite another and different thing to train a future teacher in the art of imparting such instruction to others. Hence a necessary training, to attain approved and satisfactory results in teaching. Required in Bible-Music Course. Value, 2 term hours.

Regulations

Enrollment Irregularities—A fee of $2.00 will be charged all who present themselves for enrollment on other days than those set apart for that purpose. After the days of registration a fee of $0.50 will be charged for any change in enrollment, except where such change is made necessary by action of the school. A charge of $1.00 will be made for any change in financial agreement. If by Faculty action a student is permitted to carry more than the maximum 18 periods, a charge of $1.50 per term hour is made.

Changing Courses. A change in subjects may be made by the Registrar during the first three weeks of any term, but after that, only by action of the Faculty. The Faculty reserves the right to withdraw any elective course for any term if it is elected by fewer than five students.

Transcript of Credits—At the close of the second term the Institute will supply the student with a copy of the credits earned during that school year. A charge of $1.00 will be made for subsequent transcripts of credits.

Class Absence—Each absence from class immediately

preceding or following a holiday or recess will count double. A student who absents himself from a class for more than one-eighth of its recitations shall be subject to penalty or special examination. Three tardies will be counted as an absence.

RESERVATIONS—In order to secure the assignment of a room, each applicant after receiving a letter of acceptance, should make a deposit of $2.00. No room will be reserved nor work promised to any student until this deposit has been received. It will not be refunded in any case, yet it will be credited on the cost of room and board after the student arrives.

CONDUCT—In an institution of this kind the regulation of conduct becomes necessary for the welfare of the group and the proper safeguard of the student. For this purpose a set of rules and regulations has been formulated to which the student is expected to conform. The desire of the Institute is to provide an atmosphere most conducive to reverent study and development of strong Christian character. The regulation of behavior is directed toward this end.

DRESS—It is our belief that vulgar clothes, which include those which are too elaborate for the occasion as well as those which are sleeveless or extreme in style, are not in keeping with the Christian standard of living and therefore are not acceptable for our students.

CARE OF ROOMS—Each student is responsible for the cleanliness and tidiness of his room. In addition to regularly cleaning his room he is expected to give it a thorough cleaning in the spring at the time designated by the House-keepers.

HEALTH—It is recognized that the most efficient student is the one who is healthy. Recreation periods, distinct from study periods, are provided; and every student is required to spend at least one period in the open air each day. The Institute is situated in a beautiful, shady campus equipped with some athletic apparatus.

All cases of illness are to be reported promptly to the House-keepers or the Dean. The Institute provides care for those who may have minor sicknesses.

Expenses

Board and Room _____$ 5.50 per week
Tuition for boarding students (except in Bible-
    Music Course) _____ 15.00 per term

Tuition for boarding students in Bible-
   Music Course _____ 45.00 per term
Tuition for day students _____ 25.50 per term
Tuition for day students in Bible-Music Course 52.00 per term
Registration fee _____ 1.00 per term
Library fee _____ 1.00 per term

In addition to the payment of $5.50 per week for board, room, and laundry, the student is expected to assist in the housework of the Institute about one hour each day.

Each term has seventeen weeks. Tuition must be paid at the opening of each term. Board and room should be paid monthly in advance. Any deviation from the regular time of making payments must meet with the approval of the Finance Committee.

When the dormitories are not crowded single rooms may be had by paying fifty cents extra per week.

The Institute cares for the laundry of sheets, pillow slips, towels, napkins, and a limited amount of personal laundry.

Students remaining for Christmas vacation will be charged at the regular rate of $5.50 per week. Those absent will be required to pay room rent at the rate of $1.50 per week. No deductions of board expenses will be made on absences of less than a week, and no deduction will be made on any tuition fee for which credit is given. No deductions will be made for absences of day students. A moderate charge will be made for diplomas.

Private music lessons are given to other than Bible-Music students at the following rates: one term of 15 lessons, $15.00; one term of 15 lessons, including the use of piano for one-half hour's practice each day, $17.25; one term of 15 lessons, including the use of piano for one hour's practice each day, $19.50.

To accommodate local students desiring to take one or more subjects a flat rate is made as follows: $5.00 for one term hour subject, $8.00 for a two term hour subject, and $10.00 for a three term hour course. Tuition charges are made only when a person has enrolled as a student. Anyone is welcome merely to attend lectures.

The Institute is seeking to assist students who find it necessary to do work to help meet their expenses while in training, by holding as many classes in the forenoon as possible, thus permitting students to work in the city during the afternoon. Many have earned a considerable share of their expenses in this way. However, those who must devote considerable time to secular work are encouraged to spread their course over a longer period of time. It is possible for a number of girls to work in private homes in exchange for room and board. An advance payment of $2.00 must be made by such students for home reservations, in lieu of the fee for room reservation required of resident students.

There is an opportunity for a limited number of students to pay for part of their expenses by assisting in the housework of the Institute. Those who desire such assistance should communicate with the Registrar as early as possible.

Equipment

The rooms are furnished with bedsteads, tables, chairs, and dressers, but students furnish rugs, window curtains, dresser and table scarfs, pictures, or any other articles they may desire to make the room homelike.

Each dormitory student is expected to bring a pair of blankets, comforter, bedspread, pillow, change of sheets, pillow slips, towels, and three napkins, all plainly marked on the right side with the owner's name in indelible ink. Payson's ink is recommended.

Textbooks and supplies are carried in the bookroom, and are sold at economical rates. Bibles are handled at reduced prices.

General Information

Fort Wayne is easily accessible from most points. The Pennsylvania, Nickel Plate, New York Central, and Wabash lines enter Fort Wayne. To reach the Bible Institute from any of the numerous steam and electric lines, take a South Wayne electric car to Rudisill Boulevard.

Information of any kind is given cheerfully on request. Catalogues are mailed free to anyone who may desire them. Applications for admission will receive prayerful attention. Use regular application blanks whenever convenient. If you do not have one, write for it, and it will be sent at once. Satisfactory arrangements should always be made with the Registrar before coming as a student. All applicants are advised to enter the school at the opening of the first or second term because it is very difficult to grasp a subject after the class has advanced.

Visitors are welcome at any time.

Address all inquiries concerning the courses of study, catalogues, application blanks, etc., to Registrar, Bible Institute, Fort Wayne, Indiana.

Lightning Source UK Ltd.
Milton Keynes UK
UKHW020217030119
334668UK00005B/186/P